THE BEST ME! SHARING

# Superheroes Share

by
Kimmie Auntie

Illustrations by
Ayeshe Sadr & Ishaan Dasgupta

another title brought to you from
the BEST ME series



**SCHOLASTIC**
New York Toronto London Auckland
Sydney New Delhi Hong Kong

*For my brothers and sisters, who I had to share everything but my Christmas Fruit Loops with ... and now know the happiest childhood times were hours shared with them. Glad we still get to share!*

Published by Scholastic India Pvt. Ltd.
A subsidiary of Scholastic Inc., New York, 10012 (USA).
*Publishers since 1920*, with international operations in Canada, Australia, New Zealand, the United Kingdom, India, and Hong Kong.



For information regarding permission, write to:
Scholastic India Pvt. Ltd.
A-27, Ground Floor, Sigma Centre
Infocity-1, Sector 34, Gurgaon 122001 (India)

First edition: August 2016

ISBN-13: 978-93-86106-38-4

This Reprint edition, November 2024

Printed at Sterling Graphics Pvt. Ltd., Manesar

Dear friend,

The thing is—I had to learn to like sharing. I have a lot of siblings so I shared a room, clothes, cars, parents, food, friends, everything. I would kidnap my Mom, pull her into a room and lock the door so I had a few minutes when I did NOT have to share her ... even if the other kids were banging from the other side.

I actually use to dream of a time when I did not have to share.

And then I learned something really BIG—a warm glow of happiness comes from sharing. Yup, it's true. You can try it out. Look around and be a Sharing Superhero! Share with your sibling. Share with your friends. Scout for people to share with who have less than you do ... and share sneakily so they never know it was you! Share with people you don't know. Share kindness with everyone. Just share.

Truly,
Kimmie Auntie

BOUNCE
BOUNCE
BOUNCE
BOUNCE

Max was bouncing about his house.

"Today is the daaaay!
Today is the daaaay!"

Mum teased, "Max—I know superheroes are very active. But you are extra bouncy today! What's going on?"

Max stopped bouncing long enough to twirl.

"My cousin Jack
is coming from America—
**wahoo!**

We are going to race cars, build humongous towers and knock them over. I am even going to teach Jack to play cricket!"

Bounce! Bounce! Bounce!

Dingdong!

Max dashed to the door,

"Jack! Let's go play!"

Max showed Jack his dump truck and stone collection and sling shot. Max pulled Jack outside to jump on the trampoline and pulled him inside to pet the dog. He let Jack knock over the big tower he had built and then they built a new one together. He even hollered out the window to the neighbour,

"Hey, this is my cousin, Jack!"

Max was very excited to play with his cousin.

Then Jack saw Max's favourite toy—
his super-dooper roaring walking tail-wagging
Ved the Velociraptor dinosaur.

"Hey! What's this?"

Jack reached
to pull it
down ...

bellowed Max.

But the Velociraptor was already in Jack's hand.

"GIVE THAT BACK! IT'S MINE!" yelped Max.

"But I just want to see it roar," explained Jack.

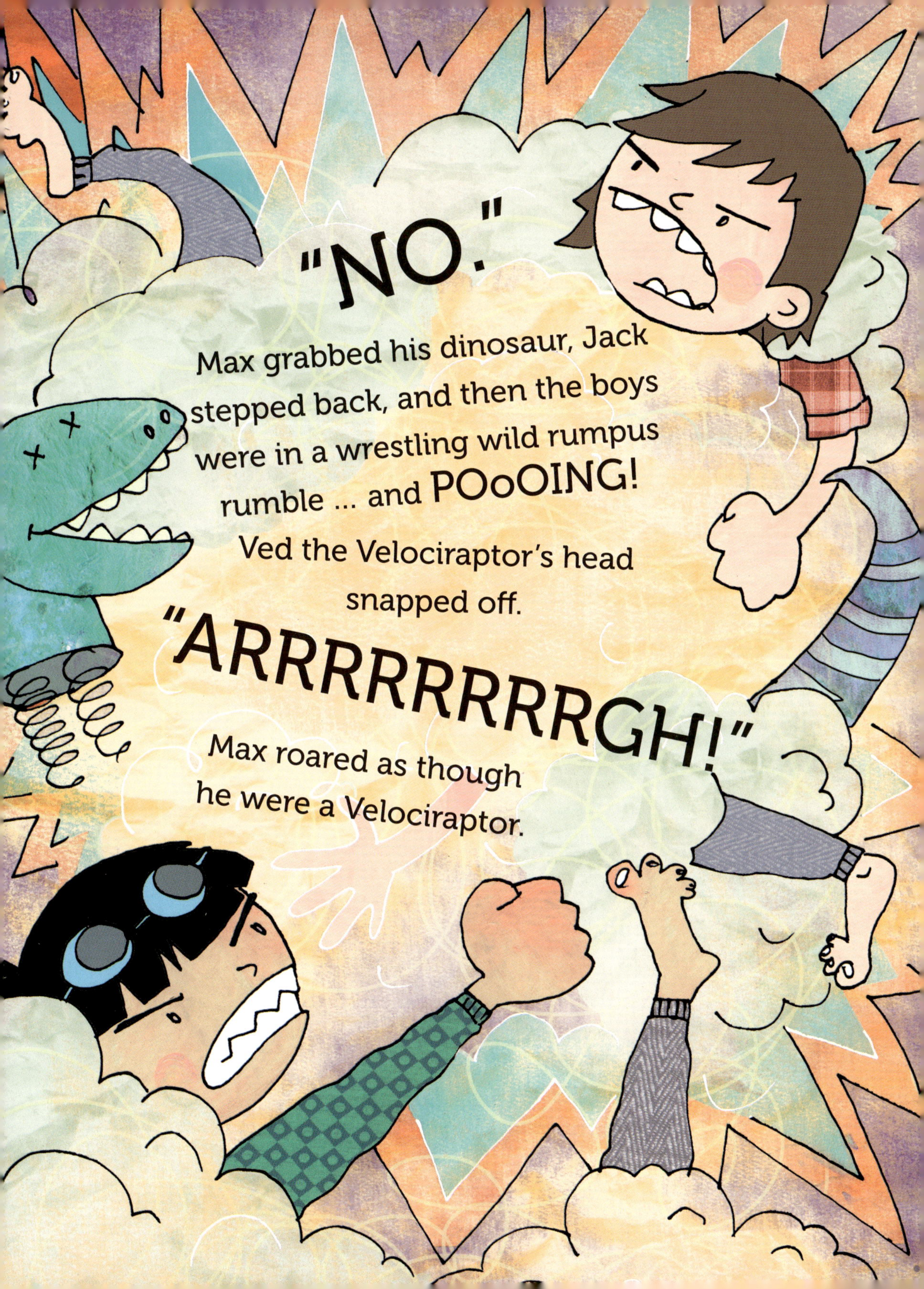

"NO."

Max grabbed his dinosaur, Jack stepped back, and then the boys were in a wrestling wild rumpus rumble ... and POoOING! Ved the Velociraptor's head snapped off.

"ARRRRRRRRGH!"

Max roared as though he were a Velociraptor.

Mum came in,

"What's all the fuss about?"

Max howled,

"He ruined my favourite toy!"

And Jack yelled,

"He wouldn't share with me!"

Mum nodded. "Time-out, boys. It seems you have forgotten that you love each other more than you love your toys. Put your arms around each other until you remember!"

The boys sat.

And sat.

A...a...a...a...nd sat.

But just sitting was very boring.

So ...

soon ...

Max leaned over,
"Hey Jack—
you want to hear
my favourite joke?"

Jack nodded.

"What's the last thing that goes through a bug's mind before it hits the windshield?"

Jack shrugged. "I don't know."

"It's bum!" Max gleefully whispered.

Jack started snickering. "Good one! Let me tell you my favourite!"

"Why is a mummy afraid of the dark?...

He has no guts!"

Max held his belly as he laughed.
"Ha ha! Tell me another one!"

Soon the boys were giggling, and whispering,
and snickering as they traded jokes.

Then Max sat up suddenly.

"Sh ... if Mum hears us she will know we are having fun in time-out!" whispered Max.

Jack added. "Let's not get caught. Sharing is more fun than fighting."

The boys grinned at each other, high-fived, and patched the Velociraptor together.

Ved the Velociraptor roared
and walked and waggled his tail.
And Mum just smiled at her two
Sharing Superheroes.

## Discussion Questions for Parents and Teachers

Why is it important to share with others?
How does it make you feel when you share with someone?
Who can we share with?
How can we find others less fortunate than us to share with?

## Activities

1. Place a variety of small items in a bag. Ask the child to close his/her eyes and reach in to take one. Discuss each item one by one. How many people can enjoy this (name of item) if I use it by myself? How many people can enjoy it if I share it? What are the ways I can share it?

2. Cooking is a great way for children to learn to share. They can take turns adding ingredients, learn to divide the finished food, and take turns eating! If you want to encourage "fair" sharing of snacks, make one child divide the portions and get the other to pick. Obviously the first child will have great incentive to make the portions even!

3. Sort clothes, toys and books with your child and let them decide what to give to others less fortunate than them. Find a meaningful way to share—but make sure your child is part of that process as well. Anonymous sneaky drops are always fun! You could even wear masks to hide your identity and provide an extra dose of delight for the kids.

## *Parenting Tip:

It is ok if your child does not want to share everything. Make a certain toy a "share only if you want to" thing. Put the toy away before friends come to play. If your child wants to share, they can take it out themselves. When your child does choose to share any toy, make sure to praise her so they learn from positive reinforcement as well.